# Minstrels and Psalmists

*Joi Darlene*
*From [illegible] A Bus*
*God Bless You!*

# Minstrels and Psalmists

*The Key to Davidic Praise and Worship*

Niles Bess

*AuthorHouse*™
*1663 Liberty Drive*
*Bloomington, IN 47403*
*www.authorhouse.com*
*Phone: 1-800-839-8640*

*© 2011 by Niles Bess. All rights reserved.*

*No part of this book may be reproduced, stored in a retrieval system, or transmitted by any means without the written permission of the author.*

*First published by AuthorHouse    05/26/2011*

*ISBN: 978-1-4634-1132-9 (sc)*
*ISBN: 978-1-4634-1133-6 (ebk)*

*Library of Congress Control Number: 2011908993*

*Printed in the United States of America*

*Any people depicted in stock imagery provided by Thinkstock are models, and such images are being used for illustrative purposes only. Certain stock imagery © Thinkstock.*

*This book is printed on acid-free paper.*

*Because of the dynamic nature of the Internet, any web addresses or links contained in this book may have changed since publication and may no longer be valid. The views expressed in this work are solely those of the author and do not necessarily reflect the views of the publisher, and the publisher hereby disclaims any responsibility for them.*

# Contents

**Introduction** .................................................................. vii

**Chapter 1** ....................................................................... 1

   Minstrels and Musicians ................................................ 1

**Chapter 2** ....................................................................... 5

   The Function of a Minstrel ............................................. 5

**Chapter 3** ..................................................................... 15

   Singers And Psalmists ................................................... 15

**Chapter 4** ..................................................................... 17

   The Function of A Psalmist .......................................... 17

**Chapter 5** ..................................................................... 25

   12 Points of The Order of Psalmists & Minstrels .... 25

**Chapter 6** ..................................................................... 37

   The Worshiper's Prayer ............................................... 37

# INTRODUCTION

When Elisha needed to hear clearly from God, he called upon the "minstrel" to adjust the atmosphere and make it conducive for the spirit of God to dwell. When the minstrel plays, it releases a frequency naturally and spiritually that charges the atmosphere with the presence of God. When we read about the mighty miracles and strong prophetic utterances of the prophets in the Old Testament, most Christians don't believe that we can still access God in that same manner or with that same level of accuracy.

Those assigned to minister in the tabernacle were also part of the ordained priesthood. When being part of the priesthood, you had to study the laws and ways of God in order to function in the temple. This process took years of training and development. The more seasoned priests would mentor the young priest to help ensure that the proper knowledge was passed down to the next generation. Because the training and development was so intense, it caused the priests to know God in a way like no other Israelite. The main ingredient here is "relationship". God had a special relationship with those in the priesthood because of the way they pursued him and sought after him.

In this book, God wants to show us that we are part of that royal priesthood and that we are a holy nation with the ability to access his presence like never before. Through the ministry of prayer, praise and worship, psalmists and minstrels can help usher in an atmosphere that's charged with the tangible presence of the Lord. The more time we spend with the father, the more his glory can shine on the inside of us that men would be drawn by His spirit. My prayer for all those that are called to the ministry of the minstrel and psalmist is *"That the God of our Lord Jesus Christ, the Father of glory, may give unto you the spirit of wisdom and revelation in the knowledge of him and the eyes of your understanding being enlightened; that ye may know what is the hope of his calling, and what the riches of the glory of his inheritance in the saints."*

**Ephesians 1:17-18**

# CHAPTER 1

## Minstrels and Musicians

Definition:
**Musician**—One who composes, conducts or performs music.

**Minstrel**—to play or strike strings, play a stringed instrument; a musician/player with the grace and anointing to move the hand of God when they play.

**1 Samuel 16:23**

²³ And it came to pass, when the evil spirit from God was upon Saul, that David took an harp, and played with his hand: so Saul was refreshed, and was well, and the evil spirit departed from him.

*II Kings 3:15* But now bring me a minstrel. And it came to pass, when the minstrel played, that the hand of the Lord came upon him.

## What is the difference?

A musician should be skilled* and a minstrel must be skilled and anointed**.

* **Skill**—Proficiency, facility, or dexterity that is acquired or developed through training or experience. An art, a trade, or a technique, particularly one requiring use of the hands or body. A developed talent or ability.

** **Anointed**—To apply oil or ointment to the head or the person. Kings were **anointed** to their office by the prophets (1 Sam. 10: 1; 1 Sam. 16: 13; 2 Sam. 5: 3; 1 Kgs. 1: 39; 1 Kgs. 19: 16; 2

Kgs. 9: 3, 6; 2 Kgs. 11: 12; 1 Chr. 11: 3; 1 Chr. 29: 22; 2 Chr. 23: 11).

The **anointing** of the priests is outlined in Ex. 40: 15; of the high priest (Aaronic order) in Lev. 21: 10. Elisha was to be **anointed** a prophet by Elijah (1 Kgs. 19: 16).

> *I Chronicles 25:1-6 {Moreover David and the captains of the host separated to the service of the sons of Asaph, and of Heman, and of Jeduthun, who should prophesy with harps, with psalteries and with cymbals: and the number of workmen\* according to their service was: the sons of Asaph, which prophesied according to the order of the king. The sons of Jeduthun who prophesied with a harp, to give thanks and praise to the Lord. The sons of Heman, the king's seer in the words of God, to lift up the horn. All these were under the hands of their father for song in the house of the Lord, with cymbals, psalteries, and harps, for the service of the house of God, according to the king's order to Asaph, Jeduthun, and Heman.*

* **Workmen**—those who perform manual or industrial labor for wages.

Both the minstrel and musician functions are extremely important to the Davidic worship design. There are different levels in rankings of minstrels/musicians. Regardless of your rank or level, you should aspire to the highest form of worship which is "obedience".

Stringed instruments are extremely important in the arsenal of the minstrel. The presence of God moves upon the strings as they are played or struck.

# CHAPTER 2

## The Function of a Minstrel

<u>2 Kgs. 3: 15</u> But now bring me a ª**minstrel**. And it came to pass, when the **minstrel** played, that the ᵇ<u>hand</u> of the LORD came upon him.

Minstrels are very strategic in the body of Christ. They have the grace and ability to unlock mysteries and loose judgment over God's enemies as they play. This is one of the key reasons why God positioned them to go "before" the armies were released into battle.

## 2 Chronicles 20: 20-24

[20] And they rose early in the morning, and went forth into the wilderness of Tekoa: and as they went forth, Jehoshaphat stood and said, Hear me, O Judah, and ye inhabitants of Jerusalem; Believe in the LORD your God, so shall ye be established; believe his prophets, so shall ye prosper.

[21] And when he had consulted with the people, he appointed singers unto the LORD, and that should praise the beauty of holiness, as they went out before the army, and to say, Praise the LORD; for his mercy endureth for ever.

[22] And when they began to sing and to praise, the LORD set ambushments against the children of Ammon, Moab, and mount Seir, which were come against Judah; and they were smitten.

[23] For the children of Ammon and Moab stood up against the inhabitants of mount Seir, utterly to slay and destroy them: and when they had made an end of the inhabitants of Seir, every one helped to destroy another.

> [24] And when Judah came toward the watch tower in the wilderness, they looked unto the multitude, and, behold, they were dead bodies fallen to the earth, and none escaped.

God is restoring the ministry anointing of the minstrel back into the Body of Christ.

## Preparation

Preparation is absolutely necessary in order to function completely as a minstrel. You must be willing to put in the necessary time during the week in order hear God's direction clearly and accurately. This includes but not limited to Fasting, Prayer, Study of the Word, Private praise and worship.

A minstrel or musician must not despise the amount of preparation. It's important that they allow the gift, talent and grace to develop completely and come to full maturation. They must be willing to put in the time to train, practice and perfect that which God has graced them with.

## Carrying the Burden of the Lord

God gave David a divine design of worship ministry in the tabernacle. The minstrels and psalmists were in charge of the song service and were responsible for communicating what God wanted to say in the service. In other words, minstrels and psalmists need to be able to hear what the spirit of the Lord is staying to the church and deliver that message. Proper preparation is key in being able to handle this responsibility.

As a psalmist and minstrel myself, I've learned through the school of the holy spirit how to function in this grace. When preparing for a service or conference, God will release his heart to me for that occasion. I then have a responsibility to release that burden and communicate his heart in that service. The key component is making yourself "available" to hear His voice! So many times I've seen worshippers move to the front and grab the microphone to release a prophetic song because the anointing is high. Once they began to sing, you could sense the anointing start to diminish. I asked the Lord during one of these occasions, "what's happening?". He told me that "I'm not speaking this right now".

When we step out to prophesy in song without the burden of the Lord upon us for that service, It's possible to grieve the spirit of God. I know that we prophesy in part and by faith but if we are not hearing His voice, we shouldn't grab the microphone. To whom much is given much is required.

## Leading the "flow" of the Minstrels/Musicians

In many of our services today, we sing an "A" and "B" selection and right when God is ready to show up and speak, we end the song and shut the flow down. It's like we are playing "ding dong ditch (running to someone's door, ringing the doorbell and then running off with God when all he wants to do is simply answer when we call. Many of us as worship leaders fail to realize that the learned song is simply a launching board into the "Flow of God".

*John 7: 38*
[38]He that believeth on me, as the scripture hath said, out of his belly shall flow rivers of living water.

Flow; rhe'-ō *(Strong's G4482)* = to flow; down; to move along in a stream; to stream or well forth; to issue or proceed from a source; to proceed continuously and smoothly; to rise and advance; as the tide; to cover with water; flood

> River; po-tä-mo's *(Strong's G4215)* = a stream, a river, a torrent, the greatest abundance, flood.

The minstrel is responsible for creating the flow. This can only be done by the holy spirit as John 7:38 clarifies for us the source of the flow. The living water is representative of the Word of God. If we are not reading and studying the word, there will be nothing there to allow the "river to flow". If your well is dry, God can't flow through you. When the minstrel has established the flow, it should be continuous. In that continuous flow, the anointing should rise and advance as the tide or as a flood. In other

*Minstrels and Psalmists*

words, the water levels of the anointing should increase as the minstrels play.

The minstrel should always be open and sensitive to when the flow should be implemented in the service. A common scenario of when the flow should be applied is at the end of a learned song or sometimes at the beginning of the service. Knowing when to shift from one flow to another is also very important.

In a company of minstrels, there should be a captain or a lead minstrel that is directing the flow. This position is also referred to as the chief musician or the chief minstrel. Shifting and moving the music takes skill and advanced abilities in playing instruments. The chief musician should be able to clearly communicate changes to the entire band so that the flow isn't broken and it remains continuous as it builds into a giant wave and floods the sanctuary with the glory of the Lord.

## Releasing Sounds from Heaven

Sound is a traveling wave which is an oscillation of pressure transmitted through a solid, liquid, or gas, composed of frequencies within the range of hearing and of a level sufficiently strong to be heard, or the sensation stimulated in organs of hearing by such vibrations.

Frequency refers to the rate at which a repeating event occurs, such as the full cycle of a wave.

I can write a whole book on this subject alone. Minstrels should always be open to hearing new sounds and musical interpretations. The important thing to remember is that releasing the new sound doesn't necessarily mean a new "keyboard" sound. It's articulating what you are hearing from heaven and translating it in a new chord pattern, vocal arrangement, dynamics, melody line, etc. All of these components make up the "New Sound".

While ministering in a Sunday service, we began to flow prophetically. We were in a familiar key using familiar chord progressions as the psalmist began to sing. The night before,

I was playing before the Lord and used some chord progressions that I had not used before that moment. I remembered those chords while we were in the prophetic flow so I began to play them. As soon as I started to play those chord progressions, the anointing and the presence of the Lord increased dramatically! I was amazed at what God was doing with such a simple adjustment in the music. That's just one example but we should press for innovation and creativity in all that we do in music ministry.

The chief musician also has to stay sensitive to know that even though they are highly skilled, sometimes the Holy Spirit wants to break the atmosphere on one simple sustained note.

Frequency plays a huge part when opening the heavens. In the church today, minstrels have instruments that must have amplification in order to be heard in the service. Because of this fact, the ministry of the scribe (audio/visual) plays a big part in the minstrel's ability to communicate with their instrument. If the sound isn't set correctly, it could hinder the flow of God in the service.

> **Ephesians 2**
> *1you hath he quickened, who were dead in trespasses and sins;2in time past ye walked according to the course of this world, according to the prince of the power of the air, the spirit that now worketh in the children of disobedience:*

The enemy is also known as "the prince of the power of the air". Because of this, he has the ability to impact and disrupt the frequencies that flow through the air. But with the power and grace of God, we pierce through the blockage and ascend in praise and worship unto the Lord Jesus Christ. We must remember who we are and walk in the dominion God has already given us.

# CHAPTER 3

## SINGERS AND PSALMISTS

Singer = A person who sings is called a singer or vocalist. Singers perform music known as songs that can either be sung *a cappella* (without accompaniment) or accompanied by musicians and instruments ranging from a single instrumentalist to a full symphony orchestra or big band.

Psalmist = A writer or composer of psalms. "David was called The Psalmist because he is believed to be the author of the Book of Psalms".

Composer—someone who composes music as a profession.

## The Difference Between a Singer and a Psalmist

Singers simply sing a song as it is written. They do their part only. Psalmists not only sing but they compose and write music/psalms. Psalmists are able to hear what God is saying and communicate it in song.

# CHAPTER 4

## The Function of A Psalmist

### Preparation

No one wrote more psalms than David. God called David "a man after His own heart". I believe one of the greatest keys to releasing the song of the Lord is the condition of the heart. God is seeking those in the earth that are worshiping him in spirit and in truth.

The preparation for a psalmist is very similar to that of the minstrel and is absolutely necessary in order to function completely. You must be willing to sacrifice during the week in order hear God's direction clearly and accurately. This includes but is not limited to fasting, prayer, study of the word and private time in praise and worship.

When psalmists take the time to cultivate their gift and anointing, it enhances their ability to precisely communicate the heart of God.

# Releasing God's Prophetic Word through Song

### Song of the Lord
*{God singing to us}*

The song of the Lord is a spontaneous, prophetic utterance in song whose composition is attributed to the inspiration of the Holy spirit. It is often released as part of a corporate expression of prophetic worship or unrehearsed worship. When we are singing the Song of the Lord, we are revealing Jesus Christ.

*Exodus 15:2*

²*The LORD is my strength and song, and he is become my salvation: he is my God, and I will prepare him an habitation; my father's God, and I will exalt him*

## Song of the Bride
*{us singing to God}*

## Harp & Bowl
*{singing the scriptures}*

Its name derived from Revelation 5:8—is a type of worship. It is music that is integrated into prayer, the "harp" representing the music and the "bowl" symbolizing the prayer of the saints (Christians) that are constantly going up like incense before the throne of God. In other words, prayer that is sung or spoken along with music.

## Song of Declaration
*{Prophetically and apostolically declaring God's Word}*

Declaration=the act of declaring; announcement: something that is announced, avowed

## Song of Proclamation
*{When you are proclaiming who God is publicly}*

Proclamation=something that is proclaimed; a public and official announcement.

## Song of Deliverance
*{When you sing songs of deliverance over a situation}*

*Psalm 32:7-8*
*[7]Thou art my hiding place; thou shalt preserve me from trouble; thou shalt compass me about with*

*songs of deliverance. Selah. ⁸I will instruct thee and teach thee in the way which thou shalt go: I will guide thee with mine eye.*

# Songs of Prayer & Supplication
{Singing prayers}

*Ephesians 6:18-20*

*¹⁸Praying always with all prayer and supplication in the Spirit, and watching thereunto with all perseverance and supplication for all saints; ¹⁹And for me, that utterance may be given unto me, that I may open my mouth boldly, to make known the mystery of the gospel, ²⁰For which I am an ambassador in bonds: that therein I may speak boldly, as I ought to speak.*


*Psalm 86:5-7*

*⁵For thou, Lord, art good, and ready to forgive; and plenteous in mercy unto all them that call upon thee. ⁶Give ear, O Lord, unto my prayer; and attend to the voice of my supplications. ⁷In the day of my trouble I will call upon thee: for thou wilt answer me.*

## Songs of Warfare
*{Songs that spiritually comes against the enemy}*

*2 Chronicles 20:22-24*
*²²And when they began to sing and to praise, the Lord set ambushments against the children of Ammon, Moab, and mount Seir, which were come against Judah; and they were smitten.sss23 For the children of Ammon and Moab stood up against the inhabitants of mount Seir, utterly to slay and destroy them : and when they had made an end of the inhabitants of Seir, every one helped to destroy another.s24 And when Judah came toward the watch tower in the wilderness, they looked unto the multitude, and, behold, they were dead bodies fallen to the earth, and none escaped.*

Our worship and praise confuses the enemy so that his attack becomes self-destructive. When we praise God in the face of a crisis we bring Him onto the battlefield, because He literally inhabits those praises. (Psalm 22:3) Thus it is He who sets up the "ambushment" on our behalf. Our victory is assured by the blood of the Lamb and the word of our testimony. (Revelation 12:11)

*Psalm 47 says that we are to "shout unto God with the voice of triumph."* Not all music is for adoration of the Lord. Some music should be specifically constructed to declare the victory we have in Christ Jesus.

# CHAPTER 5

# 12 POINTS OF THE ORDER OF PSALMISTS & MINSTRELS

### 1. PSALMISTS AND MINSTRELS WERE APPOINTED IN THEIR ASSIGNMENTS

(I Chr 16:9, 23; 15:16-28/ II Chr 20:21)

**1 Chronicles 15:16-17:**
[16]And David spake to the chief of the Levites to appoint their brethren to be the singers with instruments of musick, psalteries and harps

> *and cymbals, sounding, by lifting up the voice with joy. ⁱ⁷So the Levites appointed Heman the son of Joel; and of his brethren, Asaph the son of Berechiah; and of the sons of Merari their brethren, Ethan the son of Kushaiah;*

They were assigned an office, ordained, equipped for this function. In 2 Chronicles 20:21, the word "appointed" means "to cause to stand." We must be willing to wait on our appointment when it comes to worshiping in the house of the Lord. So many believers rush to become a part of the worship ministry without doing what is required to develop the gift God has given them.

## 2. Psalmists and minstrels had a Leader

### (I Chr 15:22, 27)

**1 Chronicles 15:22:**
> ²²*And Chenaniah, chief of the Levites, was for song: he instructed about the song, because he was skilful.*

Chenaniah, which interpreted means "preparation, made by God, favor of God" was chosen to be the Master of the Song ( Music Director). He led the entire worship ministry and they were taught under his hand.

## 3. Psalmists and minstrels were separated/set apart

## (I Chr 25:1)

### *1 Chronicles 25:1*
*¹Moreover David and the captains of the host separated to the service of the sons of Asaph, and of Heman, and of Jeduthun, who should prophesy with harps, with psalteries, and with cymbals: and the number of the workmen according to their service was:*

The word "separated" means that they were selected and set apart to this function. The minstrels and psalmist were sanctified for the ministry of praise & worship.

## 4. Psalmists and Minstrels were Instructed

## (I Chr 25:1-7 / II Chr 23:13)

### 1 Chronicles 25:1-7:

*¹Moreover David and the captains of the host separated to the service of the sons of Asaph, and of Heman, and of Jeduthun, who should prophesy with harps, with psalteries, and with cymbals: and the number of the workmen according to their service was:2 Of the sons of Asaph; Zaccur, and Joseph, and Nethaniah, and Asarelah, the sons of Asaph under the hands of Asaph, which prophesied according to the order of the king.s3 Of Jeduthun: the sons of Jeduthun; Gedaliah, and Zeri, and Jeshaiah, Hashabiah, and Mattithiah, six, under the hands of their father Jeduthun, who prophesied with a harp, to give thanks and to praise the Lord.s4 Of Heman: the sons of Heman; Bukkiah, Mattaniah, Uzziel, Shebuel, and Jerimoth, Hananiah, Hanani, Eliathah, Giddalti, and Romamti–ezer, Joshbekashah, Mallothi, Hothir, and Mahazioth:ss5 All these were the sons of Heman the king's seer in the words of God, to lift up the horn. And God gave to Heman fourteen sons and three daughters.s6*

*All these were under the hands of their father for song in the house of the Lord, with cymbals, psalteries, and harps, for the service of the house of God, according to the king's order to Asaph, Jeduthun, and Heman.s7 So the number of them, with their brethren that were instructed in the songs of the Lord, even all that were cunning, was two hundred fourscore and eight.*

## 2 Chronicles 23:12-13:

[12] *Now when Athaliah heard the noise of the people running and praising the king, she came to the people into the house of the Lord:13 And she looked, and, behold, the king stood at his pillar at the entering in, and the princes and the trumpets by the king: and all the people of the land rejoiced, and sounded with trumpets, also the singers with instruments of musick, and such as taught to sing praise. Then Athaliah rent her clothes, and said, Treason, Treason.*

The psalmists and minstrels needed instruction in order to release what the Lord had placed in their hearts and in their spirits. They were trained in the songs of the Lord.

## 5. Psalmists and minstrels were in various ranks and degrees

## (I Chr 15:16-18)

### 1 Chronicles 15:17-18:

¹⁷*So the Levites appointed Heman the son of Joel; and of his brethren, Asaph the son of Berechiah; and of the sons of Merari their brethren, Ethan the son of Kushaiah;*

¹⁸*And with them their brethren of the second degree, Zechariah, Ben, and Jaaziel, and Shemiramoth, and Jehiel, and Unni, Eliab, and Benaiah, and Maaseiah, and Mattithiah, and Elipheleh, and Mikneiah, and Obededom, and Jeiel, the porters*

According to the structure of the hierarchy of the worship order, there were three chief musicians/minstrels. Next stood others of the "second degree" or of the second order and rank. Those serving in music ministry in the house of the Lord have their various skills and levels. In order to be effective, we must recognize this and align ourselves accordingly.

## 6. Psalmists and Minstrels were chosen by name

## (I Chr 16:37-41)

### 1 Chronicles 16:41

*[41]And with them Heman and Jeduthun, and the rest that were chosen, who were expressed by name, to give thanks to the LORD, because his mercy endureth for ever;*

Psalmist and minstrels must be chosen by the set leaders in order to function freely in their grace. Leaders must have the courage to make the proper selections and not put anyone in position before their time.

## 7. Psalmists and Minstrels were Skillful

## (I Chr 15:22 / II Chr 34:12 / Psalms 33:3)

### 2 Chronicles 34: 12

*[12]And the men did the work faithfully: and the overseers of them were Jahath and Obadiah, the*

> *Levites, of the sons of Merari; and Zechariah and Meshullam, of the sons of the Kohathites, to set it forward; and other of the Levites, all that could skill of instruments of musick.*

Those that ministered in the tabernacle had the expected and necessary abilities in singing and playing to effectively articulate what the Lord was saying in song and the music. We can't ignore this important fact.

## 8. Psalmists and Minstrels were Employed in That Work

(I Chr 9:22, 26-33 / Ezek 40:44)

### 1 Chronicles 9: 33
*[33]And these are the asingers, chief of the fathers of the Levites, who remaining in the chambers were free: for they were employed in that work day and bnight.*

## 9. Psalmists and Minstrels had Charge of the Service of Song

## (I Chr 6:31-32)

### 1 Chronicles 6:31-32

*[31] And these are they whom David set over the service of song in the house of the Lord, after that the ark had rest. [32] And they ministered before the dwelling place of the tabernacle of the congregation with singing, until Solomon had built the house of the Lord in Jerusalem: and then they waited on their office according to their order.*

When the minstrel senses a flow, they should be able to communicate that to the psalmist and vice versa. This should cause the anointing to build. (Eg . . . wave & tsunami)

## 10. Psalmists and minstrels waited on their office

## (I Chr 6:31-32 / II Chr 7:6; 35:15)

### 2 Chronicles 7:6
⁶And the priests waited on their offices: the Levites also with instruments of musick of the Lord, which David the king had made to praise the Lord, because his mercy endureth for ever, when David praised by their ministry; and the priests sounded trumpets before them, and all Israel stood.

### 2 Chronicles 35:15
¹⁵And the singers the sons of Asaph were in their place, according to the commandment of David, and Asaph, and Heman, and Jeduthun the king's seer; and the porters waited at every gate; they might not depart from their service; for their brethren the Levites prepared for them.

You have to wait on your ministry in praise and worship just as those in other areas of the body of Christ have to wait on theirs.

## 11. Psalmists and minstrels received their portions

## *(Neh 10:28, 39; 11:22-23; 12:28-47; 13:5, 10)*

### *Nehemiah 11:22-23*

*$^{22}$The overseer also of the Levites at Jerusalem was Uzzi the son of Bani, the son of Hashabiah, the son of Mattaniah, the son of Micha. Of the sons of Asaph, the singers were over the business of the house of God. $^{23}$For it was the king's commandment concerning them, that a certain portion should be for the singers, due for every day.*

### *Nehemiah 12:44-47*

*$^{44}$And at that time were some appointed over the chambers for the treasures, for the offerings, for the first fruits, and for the tithes, to gather into them out of the fields of the cities the portions of the law for the priests and Levites: for Judah rejoiced for the priests and for the Levites that waited. $^{45}$And both the singers and the porters kept the ward of their God, and the ward of the purification, according to the commandment of David, and of Solomon his son. $^{46}$For in the days*

> of David and Asaph of old there were chief of the singers, and songs of praise and thanksgiving unto God. ⁴⁷And all Israel in the days of Zerubbabel, and in the days of Nehemiah, gave the portions of the singers and the porters, every day his portion: and they sanctified holy things unto the Levites; and the Levites sanctified them unto the children of Aaron.

You should receive enough resources (*financial and spiritual*) from the Lord's storehouse in order to function in the ministry of praise and worship.

## 12. PSALMISTS AND MINSTRELS FUNCTION IN THEIR COURSES OR ASSIGNED TIMES

*(I Chr 25:1-31)*

Courses are your assigned times of praise and worship. This is an excellent model for providing opportunities for emerging praise and worship leaders to be developed as well as provide experience for the next generation of psalmists and minstrels.

# CHAPTER 6

## The Worshiper's Prayer

As an ordained minister of praise and worship in your local house, you should continually cover yourself in prayer. Here is a prayer that I would like to share and invite all that have responsibility in this area of ministry to pray:

Heavenly Father, I come to You in Jesus Christ's Holy Name. Lord God, Creator of Heaven and Earth, as Your son (daughter), I come to You, to worship You as You desire, in Spirit and in Truth. Lord God, according to John 9, You seek those who worship You and do Your will out of the love You have placed in their hearts for You. Lord create in me a clean heart, a broken and contrite heart, a right heart, repentant in all my ways. Let nothing be done in strife or vain glory, but in lowliness of mind, knowing that with You Father God, all things are possible, but with man, the flesh, they shall fall short of Your Glory.

Lord I do not come to worship just to be doing something, but I come to You out of the intimate love relationship I have with You through the Blood of Jesus Christ and the Cross. I choose to abide in the Spirit of Truth, so that I am in a continued state of fellowship and worship with You, Lord God. According to what David said in Psalms 42:1-2, "As the deer pants for the water brooks, so my soul pants for Thee, O God. My soul thirsts for You, for the Living God." Lord let this be my hearts cry. Let that fire burn ever increasingly in me. Uphold me with thy free Spirit and let God be magnified! Lord if there be any wicked way within me let it be exposed and casted out.

Lord let no murmuring, complaining, backbiting nor evil be found in me, that my life be a glory, honor and a praise unto You. Circumcise my heart. Fill me with Your Spirit, Your tender mercies and loving-kindness, that I may sing praises to You all of my days. Create in me a heart of worship for I rejoice only for You. You are my joy and the lifter of my head! Through Your Spirit, lead me in rivers of Your worship and truth. Let my hands be lifted up to You as I go through this day and my life be a living sacrifice according to Romans 12:1-2, a sweet savoring aroma Heavenly Father, I yield all that I am to You and that true praise and worship come forth from my inner man. Lord, You are worthy! I give you the highest praise and shout Hallelujah! In Jesus' mighty and matchless name, Amen.

For more information or ministry engagements,
Please contact:
Niles Bess
Email: niles.bess@gmail.com
Facebook: Niles Bess
Website: anointedsoundproductions.webs.com
Office: 708-228-2384